The Little Prince
& the Rose

Antoine de Saint-Exupéry

Popcorn
ELT
Readers

Meet ...
everyone from
The Little Prince
& the Rose

The Little Prince

This is the Little Prince. He is a boy. He lives on a small planet.

The rose

The rose comes to the Little Prince's planet.

The fox

The fox lives on Earth. He is friendly and he helps the Little Prince.

The businessman

The businessman is rich, but he has no time.

The king

The king is silly. He is king of a very small planet.

The universe

The Little Prince goes to new planets in the universe. One planet is Earth.

Before you read ...
What do you think? Is the Little Prince happy or sad?

New Words

What do these new words mean? Ask your teacher or use your dictionary.

grown-up

Grown-ups don't like playing.

count

Please **count** them.

heart

His **heart** is breaking.

flower

He is giving her **flowers**.

only

There is **only** one white cat.

person

A tall **person** and a short person

planet

Earth is a **planet**. We live on Earth.

silly

You **silly** boy!

special

He's got a **special** drink.

star

The **stars** are beautiful.

'I'm sorry!'

I'm sorry!

Verbs

Present	Past
fly	flew
think	thought

The Little Prince
& the Rose

CHAPTER ONE
The rose

The Little Prince lived on a very small planet. He had yellow hair and green trousers. He was the only person on his planet.

One day, a new flower came to his planet. The Little Prince watched it every day. He waited.

One day, the flower opened.

It was a red rose.

'You are beautiful,' the Little Prince said.

'Yes, I am beautiful,' the rose said. 'I am the only rose in the universe.'

The Little Prince looked at the flower.

'It's time for breakfast,' the rose said.
'Oh!' said the Little Prince. 'I'm sorry!'
He ran for some water.

The Little Prince loved the rose, but the rose was never happy.

'Your planet is cold,' the rose said.

'Your planet is windy,' the rose said.

The Little Prince was sad.

'I'm going away,' the Little Prince said one day.
The rose was sad.

'Aren't you angry with me?' the Little Prince asked.

'No,' she said. 'I'm sorry because I was bad. I love you. Go now! Be happy!'

'Goodbye,' the Little Prince said and he flew away.

CHAPTER TWO
New planets

The Little Prince went to new planets.

On the first new planet, there was a king. He was the only person on his planet and he was silly.

'Everyone on my planet listens to me,' the king said.

'But there's no one here,' the Little Prince said.

'Everyone in the universe listens to me,' the king said.

'No one can hear you,' the Little Prince said.

'You can hear me,' the king said.

'I am going now,' the Little Prince said.

'Go!' said the king.

And the Little Prince flew away.

'You see!' shouted the king. 'You are listening to me.'

'Grown-ups are silly!' the Little Prince thought.

On the second planet, there was a businessman. He was silly too. The businessman was the only person on his planet.

'I can't talk to you,' the businessman said. 'I haven't got time.'

'What are you doing?' the Little Prince asked.

'There are a lot of stars in the universe,' the businessman said. 'I'm counting them.'

'Why?' the Little Prince asked.

'Because they are mine,' the businessman said. 'I'm rich!'

'Grown-ups are silly!' the Little Prince thought. And he flew away.

CHAPTER THREE
Earth!

Then the Little Prince came to Earth. What did he see first? A rose garden. There were a hundred red roses in one garden.

'Hello,' the roses said.

The prince was sad. His red rose was NOT the only rose in the universe.

Then a fox came into the garden.

'Hello,' the fox said.

'Hello,' the Little Prince said. 'Can you play with me? I'm very sad.'

'I can't play with you,' the fox said. 'I don't know you. There are many little boys on this planet. You're not special to me.'

'I would like to be your friend,' the Little Prince said. 'How can I be your friend?'

'I'm going to tell you,' the fox said.

'First, sit down here,' said the fox. 'Don't look at me. Don't speak.'

The Little Prince sat down. The fox sat about five metres away and watched him.

'I'm going now,' said the fox. 'Come back to the garden at four o'clock tomorrow.'

The second day, the Little Prince came back to the garden at four o'clock.

The fox was there. He sat four metres away and watched the Little Prince.

The third day, the fox sat three metres away.

The fourth day, the fox sat next to him.

'There!' said the fox. 'Now we are friends. You are my special boy.'

Every day, they came to the garden at four o'clock.

The Little Prince thought about the red rose on his planet. He loved the rose.

'I am leaving,' he said to the fox.

The fox looked sad.

'Are you going to cry?' asked the Little Prince.

'Yes,' said the fox.

'Then why did we make friends?' said the Little Prince. 'Now you are sad.'

'I'm sad, but I'm rich too,' the fox said. 'At four o'clock, every day, I'm going to think of you. You are my special boy.'

'But you aren't going to see me again,' the Little Prince said.

'I can see you with my heart,' said the fox. 'Your rose is your special rose. You love it. Look with your heart.'

'Yes!' the Little Prince said. 'I can see my rose!'

CHAPTER FOUR
'Look with your heart!'

The Little Prince thought about grown-ups.

'Grown-ups are silly. They have a hundred roses in one garden,' he thought. 'But they don't see them. They never look with their hearts.'

And the Little Prince went back to his planet.
He went back to his rose.

THE END

FLYING

In this story, the Little Prince can fly around the universe! Let's read about flying.

In a hot air balloon

The Montgolfier brothers made the first hot air balloon. They were French. The first passengers were not people … They were animals.

The balloon flew for eight minutes. The balloon and the animals came back to Earth without problems. That was on a hot day in September 1783!

By plane

The Wright brothers made the first plane. They were American. It was in 1903, and they flew forty metres. Today, we can fly very fast in big planes. We can go at 900 kilometres an hour.

Some people don't like flying. What about you?

In a space rocket

In July 1969, three men went to the moon in a space rocket. Two of the men walked on the moon. They came home three days later.

Would you like to fly in a space rocket?

Did you know?

Pilots fly planes. All pilots learn English. They speak English when they are flying.

What do these words mean? Find out.

passenger plane   hot air balloon   space rocket

After you read

1 Match and make sentences.

a) The Little Prince's planet is —   i) the stars.

b) The red rose is   ii) on Earth.

c) No one is listening to   iii) friends.

d) The businessman is counting   iv) very small.

e) There are many red roses   v) the red rose.

f) The fox and the Little Prince make   vi) the king.

g) The Little Prince goes home to   vii) never happy.

2 Complete the sentences about the Little Prince's story.

A beautiful 1) ....**rose**....... comes to the Little Prince's planet. But the rose isn't happy so the Little Prince is 2) .... The Little Prince flies to new 3) .... He talks to a 4) .... king. He asks a rich 5) .... questions. Then the Little Prince comes to 6) .... A 7) .... helps him. The Little Prince 8) .... back to his planet and his rose.

Where's the popcorn?
Look in your book.
Can you find it?

Puzzle time!

1 Put the letters in order. Then match the words and pictures.

NUS

a) .... SUN ....

i)

SSART

b) ....

ii)

AETNLP

c) ....

iii)

RAHET

d) ....

iv)

NVRSUIEE

e) ....

v)

2 You can fly! Where do you fly?

to the Little Prince's planet ☐

to the businessman's planet ☐

to Mars ☐

your idea ....

3 Who is it?

a)

The red rose

b)

....

c)

....

d)

e)

....

....

4 What about you?

a) There's a new boy in your class. You want to be his friend. Which of these do you do?

I say funny things to him. ☐

I don't listen to him. ☐

I help him. ☐

b) What do you think? Tick two words.

A good friend is ...

beautiful ☐   funny ☐   silly ☐

rich ☐   interesting ☐   nice ☐

Imagine...

1 Look at these pictures from the story.
Say what is happening.

1

2

3

4

2 In pairs, choose a picture and write some words.

The Little Prince: Why are you counting the stars?

Businessman: Because they are my stars!

1 🎵 **Listen and read.**

The Prince finds a rose.
The rose is bad.
The Prince says goodbye.
The rose is sad.

The king has no answers.
The businessman counts the stars.
The Prince flies to Earth,
And sees with his heart.

The nice red fox
Is the Prince's friend.
The fox knows the road
To a happy end.

2 🎵 **Say the chant.**